Chain Bridge at night, Budapest Hungary

Public Tram in Budapest Hungary

Parliament building in Budapest, Hungary

Hungary parliament building, Budapest Hungary

Chain bridge, Budapest Hungary

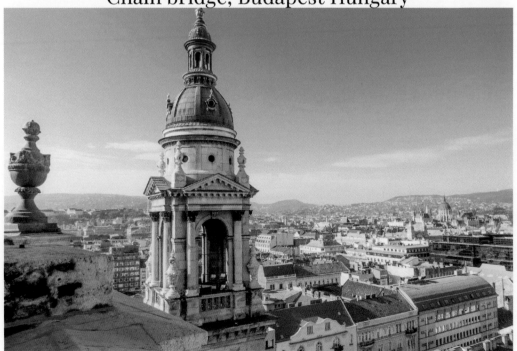

Aerial view of Budapest

Chain bridge and Hungary Parliament at Sunset

Tihany, Hungary

Hunyadi monument, Szechenyi Square Pecs Hungary

Budapest royal castle, Hungary

Traditional Hungarian soup, Goulash

National Archives of Hungary in Budapest

Lake balaton in summer, Hungary

City of Budapest

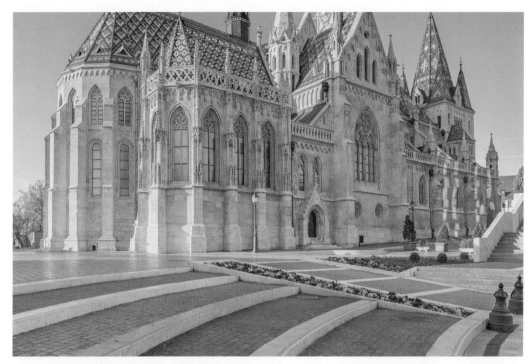

Matthias Church, Budapest Hungary

Street restaurant, Budapest Hungary

Fisherman Bastion, Budapest Hungary

Danube river, Budapest Hungary

Lavender field in Tihany Hungary

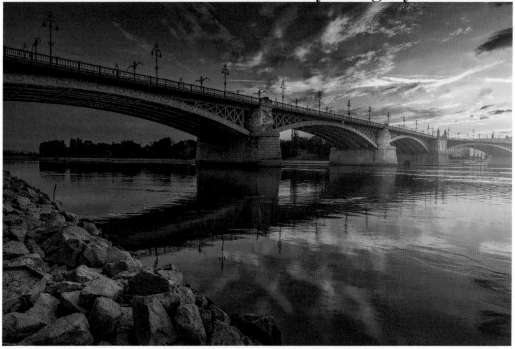

Danube Bridge at Sunset

Heroes's Square, Budapest Hungary

Szilvasvarad, Hungary

Street in Gyor, Hungary

Miskolc, Hungary

Buildings in Budapest, Hungary

Hungary's Flag

puszta horse drivers Hungary

View of Eger city Hungary

Heores Square, Budapest Hungary

Lake Balaton Hungary

Stephen's Basillica, Budapest Hungary

Rooftops of Sopron, Hungary

Szechenyi Medicinal bath, Budapest Hungary

Szombathely, Hungary

Church in Eger, Hungary

Heroes Square, Budapest Hungary

Mako, Hungary

Beautiful Hungary at sunset

Traffic at Chain Bridge, budapest Hungary

Boat on Danube river. Budapest Hungary

Boat at Budapest

Fountain at Mageret Island, Budapest Hungary

Hungary parliament, Budapest

Carmelite Baroque church, Gyor Hungary

River Danube, Hungary

Spring in Hungary

Clay house, Leshten Hungary

Saaint George Church, Sopron Hungary

lake balaton, Hungary

Hungary, Budapest

Romanesque Cathedral, Pecs Hungary

Harbor in Siofok, Hungary

Statue of Lajos, Kossuth Pecs Hungary

Budapest cityscape at night

Villany, Hungary

Cable car on Castle hill, Budapest Hungary

Budapest, Hungary

cave in Erzsebetvaros, Hungary

Esztergom, Hungary

Entrance of Hungary Parliament, Budapest

Pecs, Hungary

Tourist boat on Danube river, Hungary

Basilica of St. peter and St. paul, Cathedral, Pecs Hungary

Vineyard, Villany Hungary

budapest, Hungary

Forest at Urom, Hungary

Eger, Hungary

Budapest, Hungary

Rooftops of Sopron, Hungary

Eger, Hungary

Cathedral church in Pecs Hungary

Interior of Hungary Parliament, Budapest

Bird in Heves, Hungary

Small village of Holloko, Hungary

Budapest, Hungary

St. Stephen's Basilica, Budapest Hungary

Streets of Budapest, Hungary

Votive church, Szeged, Hungary

Petal in Szodliget, Hungary

Interior of Hungary Parliament, Budapest

Budapest street

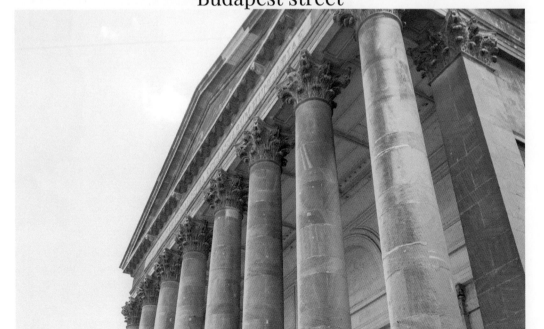

Basilica of Esztergom, Budapest Hungary

Field in Solymar, Hungary

House in Szentendre. Hungary

Landscape of Lake Balaton, Hungary

Street of Gyor Hungary

the county hall, Pecs Hungary

Hernad, Hungary

Visegrad, Hungary

Petfurdo, Hungary

Holloko Village, Hungary

Street in Sopron Hungary

The Gozsdu Courtyard, Budapest Hungary

Field in Dorog, Hungary

Budapest, Hungary

Rimoc, Hungary

Tihany, Hungary

Nagykovacsi, Hungary

Gyorujbarat, Hungary

Kaposvar main square, Hungary

Printed in Great Britain
by Amazon

21918184R00030